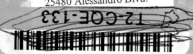

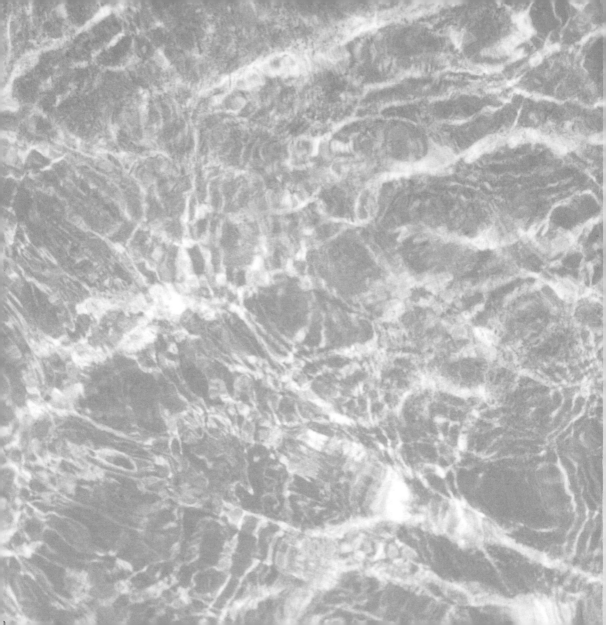

The Art of Expecting

By Véronique Vienne with photographs by Jeanne Lipsey

The Art of Expecting

SIMPLE WAYS TO MAKE ROOM FOR THE FUTURE

Clarkson Potter/Publishers
New York

Published by Clarkson Potter/Publishers, New York, New York.
Member of the Crown Publishing Group.

Random House, Inc. New York, Toronto, London, Sydney, Auckland
www.randomhouse.com

CLARKSON N. POTTER is a trademark and POTTER and colophon are
registered trademarks of Random House, Inc.

Printed in Japan

Library of Congress Cataloging-in-Publication Data
Vienne, Véronique.
The art of expecting: simple ways to make room for the future / Veronique Vienne.
Includes bibliographical references.
1. Pregnancy. 2. Childbirth. 3. Pregnant women. 4. Infants—Care. I. Title.
RG525.V525 2002
618.2'4—dc21   2001021644

ISBN 0-609-60926-2

10 9 8 7 6 5 4 3 2 1

First Edition

DEDICATION

To Emeric, Isabelle, Hugo, and Gaëtan

ACKNOWLEDGMENTS

The friends of my daughter are now becoming parents. Only yesterday I was sitting on the edge of a sandbox with them; today I am writing about their experience raising kids. I am as much in awe of their spunk and self-assurance now as I was back then, and I feel lucky to have known them so long. I am particularly indebted to the young parents who appear in this book with their children, namely Kirsten and Michael Turner, Emeric and Isabelle Pinon, Fabien and Niagalé Penone, Tony and Stacy Wolberg, Lindsay and Harley Walsh, Anne-Marie Kim and Theo Lubke, Thierry Renard and Aude Maury, Gitta Robinson and Richard Grisaru, and Patrick Boyland and Roger Hockett—with a very special thanks to my editor, Annetta Hanna, whose precious daughter, Ella, inspired me in the first place.

Also inspiring were members of our extended family—the Lipseys, the Lubtchanskys, the Kilverts, the Youngs, the Viennes, the Hoffmans, the Harpels—and many good friends and their children, including Judith Shepherd, Owen and Regina Edwards, Sean Elder and Peggy Northrop, Catherine Ettlinger and Bruce Kapson, Lygeia Grace, Penelope Rowlands, and Ward Schumaker.

And of course I want to thank all the people who babied us through the process: our agent, Helen Forson Pratt; creative director, Marysarah Quinn; Sharona Jones, who helped with the research; Vicky and Marion at Chelsea Black & White; and Seamus Mullarkey, who gave editorial advice. Last but not least, I want to pay homage to my parents—all four of them: Marc and France, Colette and Pierre. I am proud to be their child.

CONTENTS

introduction 9

1 The art of wishing 10
EXPECTING WITHOUT EXPECTATIONS 14

Family Planning 17

2 The art of conceiving 18
THE BEST DADDY EVER 22

Nine Months in the Life of a Man 25

3 The art of birthing 26
THE MIRACLE OF LOVE 30

Name Your Baby 33

4 The art of trusting 34
PREMATURE WORRIES 38

Twelve Reasons to Have Children 41

5 The art of nesting 42
CARRYING CHARGES 47

The Stuff of Memories 51

6 *The art of bustling* 52
THE ZEN OF GETTING THINGS DONE 56

Sexy Moms 59

7 *The art of soothing* 60
A NEW FEEDING FORMULA 63

Recipes for Instant Comfort 67

8 *The art of negotiating* 68
GOING WITH THE FLOW 72

Because I Say So 75

9 *The art of celebrating* 76
SHARED HAPPINESS 79

Terms of Endearment 83

10 *The art of being there* 84
THE REST OF YOUR LIFE 89

A Final Quiz 91

conclusion 93
a selected bibliography 95
photo credits 96

The only thing he expects is that
you'll be there to catch him.

Nothing can ever truly prepare anyone for the experience of giving life. Because no two situations are ever alike—each baby is born with a fiercely individualistic set of needs and wants—it's impossible to predict the future.

Though a wide range of useful information is out there for expectant mothers and fathers, you, like everyone else, will be caught off-guard by the actual demands of pregnancy, childbirth, and infant care. And you'll wonder why no one told you that it would be so hard—or so easy, depending on the case.

A benign veil of silence does indeed surround parenthood. It is a protective cocoon designed by people who have been there before you. As if by tacit agreement, parents, doctors, and even experts have decided that some things

you don't want to know. Trust them. No one can, or should, try to anticipate every possible scenario.

What you can do, though, is expect to be surprised. Most of your preconceived ideas about becoming a parent should be challenged.

In this book, you will discover, for instance, how very important men are in the birthing process. Why crying infants are not necessarily distressed. Why some worries can make us feel lucky. Why it's beneficial for babies to be cuddled as much as possible. And how doing menial housework can become as easy as eating bonbons.

The biggest surprise, of course, is that if you trust how you feel in the moment—rather than try to follow rules—your baby will be in good hands.

the art of wishing

upid is up to his old tricks again. Just when we think that we've got a handle on life, he strikes with his most mischievous arrow to date. Suddenly we turn mushy. We become prone to daydreaming. We sigh without knowing why. We get teary-eyed thinking about our childhoods. Some of us even begin to collect knickknacks that are small, round, pudgy, and smooth.

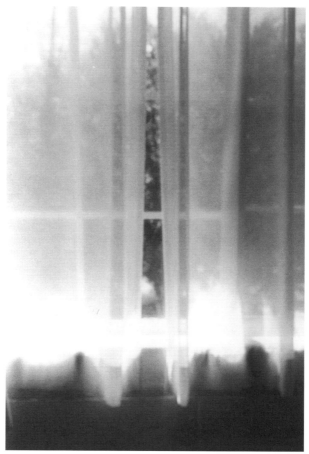

To wait—and hope—is a creative act.

We should have known better, but somehow, in the heat of passion, we overlooked that all-important detail: Cupid, the symbol of erotic love, looks soft and cuddly—like a baby. Wasn't that warning enough? No—the angelic Valentine icon is a savvy trickster. But now it's too late. We are pregnant with a secret wish still too scary to name.

Usually, you find out that you are thinking about starting a family when you begin to notice a parallel universe of chubby and colorful products that used to be hidden from your sight. Bright and cheery, child paraphernalia does not become visible until you are ready to see it. Your first discovery of all those cute and squishy objects is startling indeed.

In supermarkets, busy career women who routinely fill their carts with French Roquefort cheese and extra-virgin olive oil are unexpectedly riveted by the sight of rows of tiny jars of puréed baby food.

Impulsively, blond beauties with perfect manicures and prestigious jobs in public relations insist on hosting elaborate baby showers for the pregnant brides of their wealthy clients.

All of a sudden, athletic husbands who drive off-road vehicles and go rafting on weekends secretly envy their male friends with infant car seats in the back of their four-door sedans.

By the time we interpret these early symptoms for what they are, there is no turning back. An innate biological mechanism has taken over. Our evolutionary heritage has activated in us the urge to care for and protect someone who is a lot smaller—and a lot cuter—than we are.

The study of the endearing physical appeal of babies and its importance in the developmental process is a well-documented science called *neoteny*. The "morphology of cute," as some people call it, is first and foremost characterized by large, saucer-sized eyes. But our neurocircuitry is also sensitive to round, bulging cheeks, a small jaw, relative hairlessness, a lack of pronounced sexual differences, an absence of teeth, and elasticity of body. Anthropologists believe that these neotenic features give helpless infants a critical advantage by making them look nonthreatening to overly aggressive adults.

And so yes, we are hardwired to be smitten by babies. We go cootchie-cootchie over teething infants and are besotted by round-eyed tots. Sexual attraction may fail to trick some couples into having children, but the presence of other people's offspring clutching teddy bears and stuffed baby elephants acts as a powerful incentive for them to become parents.

Once you have acknowledged that you are ready to have children, it could be years before you finally buy the adorable crib with its matching changing table. Truth be told, a child is often conceived mentally years before the little stick of a pregnancy test turns blue or pink. The real moment of his conception can be traced all the way back to the day you felt compelled to buy a rubber ducky for your bathtub or to that time you spent a fortune on a party dress for your newborn niece.

EXPECTING WITHOUT EXPECTATIONS

Learning to expect a child—without projecting your own expectations—is the best preparation for raising kids. Patience is probably the most important quality one has to have as a parent.

Nature doesn't take orders from us. To this day, no known procedure, medical or amorous, can force a human life into existence. Medical authorities are beginning to wonder whether what we call infertility isn't just a fancy diagnosis for sheer impatience. Watched pots never boil.

Will you have a boy or girl? A sweet angel or an endearing little devil? A Pisces or a Libra? Keep guessing.

You can wish all you want, but you are not in control. Making yourself available, even though, in the end, you may not get exactly what you want, is a skill that you, as a future father or mother, should acquire as soon as possible. Why not use the time spent waiting for the good news as practice for the many instances when your child's schedule will not coincide with yours?

- When she needs to go to the bathroom and you're stuck in traffic.

- When she stays up past your bedtime.

- When he decides that he doesn't want his bottle after all, even though he was screaming for it a minute ago.

- When he develops a fever the first day you go back to work.

When it comes to kids, asserting your will is a futile exercise. Eventually you'll discover that the best way to be in charge is not to try to call the shots. Your main advantage as a parent will be neither your considerable knowledge nor your superior wisdom—scrap those. Your main advantage will simply be your size. Learn to be bigger in more ways than one. Stay on top of situations by standing up even taller. And never let down little people.

Only one thing is sure: Raising a child will require you to rise above your own expectations.

Family Planning

If you are postponing pregnancy until you are all set to have a baby, do yourself a favor: Accept the possibility that you may never start a family.

See, children love to surprise us. They hate schedules. When you are ready for them, they don't show up. When you least expect them, they butt in. So if you really want a baby, don't wait; get busy.

❈   Buy a fixer-upper on an inaccessible island.

❈   Run for office in your district.

❈   Change your career—decide to become an architect.

❈   Move into a tiny apartment in the city and study acting.

❈   Adopt twins.

❈   Open a restaurant.

Forget about your "window of peak fertility."
Throw away your ovulation tests and basal temperature charts.
You'll get pregnant when it's least convenient.

The only certainty is that we don't know who, when, and where.

2

the art of
conceiving

e take for granted
that pregnancy is first and foremost the affair of
women. This notion is about to change—and not a
moment too soon. Men, it turns out, play a greater
role in the conception of their child than was ever
thought before. In the last few years, scientists have
determined that the father's DNA is biologically
responsible for making the placenta. Maternal genes

nurture the embryo, but paternal genes provide the cocoon in which it grows. In other words, the XY cells of the vigilant dad protect the baby in the womb.

Though he is not directly concerned by the external manifestation of pregnancy, the father nevertheless goes through an uncomfortable period of incubation. Wild fluctuation of hormones triggers in him a psychosomatic process called *couvade,* which prompts him to experience baby-making as a physical event. Although it is obviously less taxing for him, the time of pregnancy is nonetheless a difficult period during which he carries his share of the physiological burden of gestation.

For starters, as soon as his wife gets pregnant, he becomes virtually invisible. Even his parents ignore him—they only want to know how *she* is doing.

Adding insult to injury, a man can never be sure that he is the rightful biolog-ical father of his baby—and, ouch, there is genetic evidence that at least one in ten dads isn't. Emotionally confused, he is prey to a multitude of unspoken anxieties.

He gets little comfort from the woman he married. She has been taken away from him, replaced by a stranger who spends hours on the phone talking to her girl-friends about "epidurals" and "episiotomies."

And overnight he is expected to stop smoking, change the litter box, memorize the obstetrician's phone number, and give up his study to make a nursery.

His health deteriorates as well. He may get sicker than his pregnant wife. He may gain more weight than she does. He may en-dure abdominal pain and leg cramps. And there is no remedy for the delicate con-dition of this wretched dad, other than cuddling at last with his newborn infant.

A baby grows in the father's psyche at about the same rate as in the mother's

Men's genes make mothers out of women.

womb. Pregnancy, it seems, helps transform women into mothers—and men into fathers. The hormonal swings in both parents prime their brains to the point where agonizing over the pros and cons of disposable diapers becomes an acceptable way to spend a romantic evening.

More than idle bystanders, pregnant men have nonetheless been ignored by the medical profession. Self-conscious and ill at ease, these chivalrous sperm-bearers have been reluctant to draw attention to their aches and pains. But a growing number of psychobiologists are now convinced that indeed a majority of parturient males suffer from indigestion, nausea, thickening waistlines, and unexpected bouts of fatigue—all symptoms of couvade, the mysterious dad-to-be ailment.

Next time you meet a father-to-be, greet him with a heartfelt "How are you doing?" Let him know that he is not alone.

Unborn babies, it seems, don't like to venture down the birth canal unless both parents are present in the room. Moms have noticed that the timing of the child's arrival is often contingent on paternal whereabouts. There is anecdotal evidence that in many instances labor doesn't start until the father shows up. It's almost as if the infant had her bags packed and was ready to go, only waiting to hear the sound of her dad's key in the door to begin her lifelong journey.

The kids are trying to tell us something—and maybe we should listen. As far as they are concerned, a matched set of parents is a critical asset. And to make sure that his father is as involved as his mother, the little critter will do his utmost to seduce the dad. A mom often watches in disbelief as her child turns on full-volume charm to melt Daddy's heart.

As babies grow, they seem to develop increasingly more sophisticated strategies to secure ongoing paternal commitment.

A father who consoles a frightened child in the middle of the night is rewarded with a big, passionate, heartwarming hug.

When he offers to take his toddler to buy shoes, the kid acts as excited as if he was about to go on a field trip to the moon.

And if ever he picks up his little girl at a friend's house after a birthday party, he becomes forever her matinee idol.

Needless to say, if parenting was judged on merit alone, mothers would get the gold medal. Don't count on it, though. Little cherubs don't play favorites based on a fair assessment of the various sacrifices each parent makes on their behalf. What kids want above all is the comfort of two caring adults, and they'll do what they have to do in order to secure the affection of both. The two-parent unit—whether it's Mom and Dad or some nontraditional combination like Papa and Pop or Mom and Auntie—offers children a double dose of safety.

The patriarchal system is under scrutiny these days, with good reasons. Yet it was originally invented for the sole benefit of the kids, to encourage fathers to stick around to protect their progeny. Mothers were responsible for giving their children life, while fathers were expected to give them a name—and with it a legal and social identity.

Today, caring for a child is a privilege two people share freely. Don't compare the contribution each of you makes to the family. Don't turn your parenting into a meritocracy. Chances are your child will love you both madly—whether or not you deserve it.

Are you man enough to cuddle a baby?

Nine Months
in the Life of a Man

In nine short months, a man must develop the new psychological organs that he will need to function as a dad. Embryonic at first, his timid involvement will little by little mature into a full-fledged paternal conscience.

* In the fourth week of his wife's pregnancy, he will begin to notice other people's kids, and he will slow down to respect speed limits.

* In the twelfth week, he will tell his friends at work that he is leaving early to go to a ball game when in fact he is taking his wife for a checkup.

* Before the twenty-fifth week is over, he will fantasize about looking manly while burping his baby.

* Toward the end of the thirty-sixth week, he will surf the Web in search of the perfect infant car seat instead of going out drinking with his buddies.

In other words, he will be well on his way to becoming the kind of father who takes his squirming daughter out of her bulky snowsuit before taking off his own coat and hat.

the art of birthing

aving a baby? Not exactly. More accurately, your baby is having you. A new life has taken possession of your body—and you are in the process of gestation. If you could, you'd curl up into the fetal position and spend the next nine months tucked away in the deep recesses of creation. Being pregnant gives you a chance to experience firsthand a world in the making.

Though conventional wisdom would have you believe that your body is expanding to make room for the developing fetus, you could swear that it's just the opposite. With each passing week, you feel that you are in fact shrinking to accommodate the growing presence of the child within you.

Don't panic. Your identity as a woman is only temporarily displaced by the mother-child symbiosis. When the time comes for your baby to give birth to the mommy he is carrying, you will both emerge from the process as two separate beings.

In the meantime, you try to assert a modicum of control over your condition by eating healthy food, avoiding harmful drugs, getting regular checkups, and reading books on pregnancy and child care. Yet no matter how hard you try, you can never be sure that you are doing the right thing. There are too many uncertainties—too many "contingencies," to use the jargon of childbirth experts. You have to find another way to prepare for the future.

You have to trust nature. Nature made human beings adaptable, which is why we are so successful as a species. What makes the biological wetware between our ears so unique is its ability to keep on learning. Instead of being hardwired in advance to deal with all foreseeable emergencies, we learn selectively, inventing solutions as we go, always curious, often playful, and forever in a state of creative expectation.

To expect is a lofty predicament. We hold pregnant women in awe because they personify this mixture of fragility and resilience that is the secret of our survival.

Savor if you can this peculiar chapter in your life during which you are all expectations. There is nothing trivial about your hopes or anxieties, whether they involve the health of your baby, the financial state of your family, the length of your maternity

That flutter inside? It's a future in a state of becoming.

leave, or the shape of your body.

The vulnerability of your baby, for instance, will put you in touch with an inner strength and an indomitable faith that you didn't know you had.

Legitimate misgivings about money will force you to reappraise your skills, streamline your expenses, and explore more efficient ways to make a living.

Childcare concerns will challenge all your assumptions about gender roles—and will give Mr. Mom a chance to gain precious hands-on experience.

And when assessing the transformation of your figure—from your magnificent tummy to your *Playboy* bosom—you'll discover the irresistible sex appeal of your newly acquired sense of humor.

THE MIRACLE OF LOVE

Nature gave us the ultimate gift of adaptation—an uncanny ability to challenge natural laws! Indeed, in order to nurture her unborn child, a mother must defy one of the most basic principles of biology: To allow the embryo to develop safely in her uterus, she has to suppress her own immunological response.

Against the biological odds, love conquers all.

In theory, the mother's body should reject the fetus as it would an organ implant. Though miscarriages do happen, in the majority of cases, maternal T cells don't fight against the genetic infiltrator. Scientists are stumped. No one knows why the father's XY cells, encoded in the embryo, are usually tolerated by the mother's pugnacious antigens.

That said, at the beginning of the pregnancy, the mother's autoimmune system does put up a bit of a struggle. During the first three months, she feels as if she has been abducted by alien chromosomes. The fertilized embryo, a tiny Trojan horse parked in her womb, is their headquarters. And no amount of morning sickness can dislodge the intruders.

If everything goes well, the mom will eventually be subdued by the ferocious determination of the cells proliferating at breakneck pace in the nave of her being. She'll learn to love the tiny guest who is usurping her hospitality.

She'll even grow proud of the selfish genes of her future child. Toward the end of her ordeal, she'll look more and more like the baby she is carrying—swaying gently as she walks, her feet receding in the domed shadow of her expectant belly.

Vase, vessel, jar, chalice, mother.

Name Your Baby

When you pick a name, you give your baby the magic password that will open the doors of his or her future.

* When naming a baby, a two-people jury is better than a committee of one. A child is less likely to be called Quasar or Hallelujah when two people in their right minds talk it out.

* If you lobby for Michael over Winslow, chances are you are the dad. When he is eight, your son will be grateful you prevailed. By the time he is in college, though, he probably will have more cachet with the girls as Winslow.

* If you know better than to name your baby girl after Aunt Gertrude, you are the mom. You don't want your daughter to be perceived as less attractive than all the fetching Caitlins, Amandas, Danielles, Tiffanys, and Ashleys out there.

* Good things happen to parents who are in complete agreement over naming their infant Barrington, Thelonious, or Regina: To overcome unusual names, squirming bundles will excel in school and make them proud.

* If your mate comes up with a pretty good suggestion—Lorelle if it's a girl, Preston if it's a boy—don't try to find something much better. Make it a done deal. The name you give your child will be synonymous with love.

With a name, a newborn becomes a person.

the art of trusting

Even the most trusting
of expectant parents are sometimes given to bouts of
intractable panic. Before we ever lay eyes on our
newborn, we already dread the thought of losing
her. We worry for a good reason. For mother and
child, parting is the prelude to meeting—the delivery
being first and foremost a wrenching process of sep-
aration. What a lousy way to start a relationship:

He'll be safe if he knows that you trust him.

You have to say good-bye before you can say hello.

During the next twenty years, you'll have to say good-bye many more times. Not just once, or twice, or even three times. No matter how much you worry in advance, or how careful you are, once the umbilical cord is cut, your child is adrift in the world.

Trust your fate, trust your child, or trust the devil if you must. No amount of supervision will ever be enough to keep your baby out of trouble.

Take for granted that you will have the fright of your life the day your toddler disappears on a crowded beach. She'll wander out of sight, leaving no footsteps in the dry sand. Twelve minutes later, when you discover her on the boardwalk, her face covered with cotton candy, you'll know that, since her birth, you've been living on borrowed time.

Three years later, you'll lose her again, this time in the New York City subway. Just before the doors of the train close, she'll jump back into the car to fetch the teddy bear she inadvertently left on her seat. You'll be standing alone on the platform, while around you everything goes dark, like the world during a solar eclipse. Seven minutes later you will be reunited at the next station, where you will find her sitting on a bench, next to a benevolent stranger, patiently waiting for you—you, a convicted mother, released on parole, yet sentenced for life.

Trust me—you'll lose your child a few more times, too: to the Cartoon Channel, to action figures, to the megaplex culture, to teen idols, and to a posse of giggling friends who stop talking when you walk into the room.

But none of it will be as traumatic as the day you lose your daughter to nascent nicotine addiction—the day you find a pack of cigarettes at the bottom of her school-bag. Of course you will confront her. To make your point, you will ceremoniously flush the cigarettes down the toilet in front of her. "How dare you touch my stuff!" your twelve-year-old will shriek. "I hate you forever!" But this time you won't let her slip through your fingers. "You've got it wrong, young lady," you'll say. "Allow me to disagree. You do not hate me. On the contrary, you love me."

There is a point, usually at the onset of puberty, when kids have to learn that differences of opinion can coexist with unconditional love. For them, this parting of the ways is a rite of passage. For us parents, it is a second birthing ritual, another wrenching ordeal during which we must push them out and away—and into the world. The Latin words *partire,* "to part," and *parturire,* "to be in labor," are very close indeed.

Surviving the first major disagreement with your daughter or son—and trusting that they will be able to handle the pressure—can take your breath away. The torment is often worse than the pain of childbirth. At that moment, you may wish you never had kids in the first place. Minutes later, though, you will realize that your children will never leave you. They are a gift—a gift no one, not even them, can ever take away from you.

PREMATURE WORRIES

In spite of our boundless capacity to torment ourselves, we can never be fully prepared for what can go wrong with our children. Because babies are still in a state of becoming when they enter the world, the potential for problems are limitless. But our worries, called "adaptive" by psychologists, help us prepare for impending changes. With questions like Will My Baby Be Healthy? and Will I Know What To Do Next? we try to map out the journey ahead.

We collect pull-out child safety guides from various parenting magazines and put them on the refrigerator door to keep away the evil eye. We install a carbon monoxide alarm in the nursery and attach a water-filtering system to the kitchen sink. We check the manufacturer's recommendations for every piece of equipment, from mattress to mobile to guardrails. And still we wake up in the middle of the night in a cold sweat shuddering at the thought of the baby swallowing the beady eyes of his teddy bear.

Bravo! say the experts. The function of our premature worries is to help us realize that we are lucky. After exploring worst-case scenarios, we have reason to be grateful. And in the light of our most dreadful expectations, we feel very fortunate.

But just as worries are part of our adaptive behavior, so are our delusions. In spite of all the scientific information that is available to future fathers and mothers today—some of it frightening—people still manage to enter the birthing room blissfully unaware of the hazards they will have to face as parents.

Good for them.

In the last analysis, no two human experiences are ever the same. What's a breeze for some turns out to be a horror story for others, and vice versa. That's why, ultimately, parents-to-be have very little patience for all the folk wisdom and expert advice that is thrust at them. Like the clueless baby they will soon hold in their arms, they are eager to discover life on their own terms.

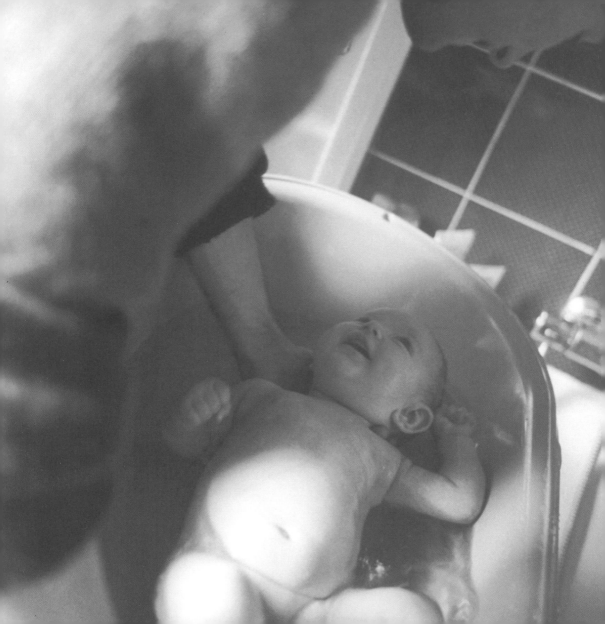

Twelve Reasons to Have Children

Why go to the trouble of having kids? Considering the tremendous investment, it hardly makes sense. Why you even bother is a question you have to figure out on your own. To get you thinking, here is a short list of options.

- ✺ You wish to pass on to posterity the best qualities of your mate.
  You wish to pass on to posterity your sense of humor.

- ✺ You need a good excuse for baking chocolate chip cookies.
  You need a good excuse for being broke.

- ✺ You love children.
  You love major disruptions.

- ✺ You'd like to give your parents a grandchild.
  You'd like to give your in-laws a chance to treat you as their child.

- ✺ You want to be the mother of his children.
  You want to be the dad of her rambunctious brood.

- ✺ You are ready to settle down.
  You are ready to learn to blow someone else's nose.

You want a child because you want to experience pure joy in your lifetime.

∽ 5 ∽

the art of nesting

A baby held against your heart is always the perfect weight, never too light or too heavy. To pick him up is the next best thing to snuggling into the most luxurious cashmere wrap. Even though you are the one doing the hugging, you feel deliciously tucked in. Your chest heaves with pleasure as you instinctively adjust the contour of your arms to fit the nooks and crannies

of the infant's diminutive curves. The muscles in your neck loosen, your spine flexes, your head bows. Soon there isn't a single straight line left in your body.

A minute ago you were just taking up space on the planet. But with a baby in your arms, you've become a berth in the universe—a niche, a nook, a nest. You were a person? You've become a place.

One would be hard-pressed to explain why it's so soothing to cradle ten pounds of wiggling and drooling humanity. Alarmingly vulnerable, babies are also deeply comforting. The nest you make for them—cheek to cheek, heart to heart, or tummy to tummy—is a safe harbor for both you and them.

This simple human contact is often the most effective way to keep a baby happy—and his parents stress-free. Researchers have established that the reason babies in "less advanced" cultures do not cry as often as kids in this country is because members of their extended family—and a coterie of older siblings—hold them for long stretches of time.

Unfortunately, here, too many of us believe that picking up a baby is synonymous with spoiling him. We are told that an infant must learn to bide his time in his crib, his infant seat, and his playpen. If we were to hoist the little tyke in the air each time he cries or frets, he might turn into an embezzler or a hoodlum.

Of course you know better. When no one is looking, you tear your child away from the pull of gravity to give him a chance to view the world from up there, five feet above the ground. Perhaps one reason birds build their nests in high places is to familiarize their brood with the sight of the earth from the sky. Likewise, we give our newborns an incentive to grow tall and stand upright each time we scoop them up in our arms.

Like birds, kids love to survey the world from a safe perch.

For years to come, you will be your kid's favorite perch. Day after day, month after month, you will develop stronger abdominal and pectoral muscles to accom-modate the increasing weight of your charge. Eventually the robust ten-year-old will feel no heavier than she did as an infant or a toddler. A benevolent giant,

Always a charge, never a burden.

you'll take for granted that you will always be able to lift her up and carry her over obstacles.

Indeed, it will be the best of times for you when your child tightens his grip around your neck and says he never wants to let you go. Don't be in a hurry to pry his little fingers apart. To hug and to hold—this sweet burden of parenting—lasts only a short decade.

CARRYING CHARGES

To explain why humans walk upright, some anthropologists have suggested that our ancestors stood up in order to hold and protect their helpless infants. Unlike newborn monkeys, who can cling to their mother's fur within minutes of their birth, human babies, with their big brains but limited physical abilities, could not possibly survive unless they were carried around all day long by dexterous and light-footed parents.

That was then. Today we have a wide range of traveling options to carry babies around: the swaddling sling, the take-along pouch, the portable bassinet, the infant seat, the backpack baby carrier, the deluxe stroller—and the latest invention, the rear-facing, five-position, one-step-folding, dual-rear-brake, adjustable-canopy baby travel system.

Good grief! The nomadic hunter-gatherer parents had an easy time compared with us. Before modern moms and dads can head for the mall with their newborn, they must lug as much state-of-the-art equipment as astronauts on a lunar landing expedition.

You'll be tempted to question the benefits of technological progress the day you have to pull open a heavy glass door while single-handedly maneuvering a full-size baby carriage with its rear swivel wheels stuck the wrong way around. On the other hand, you'll doubt the wisdom of evolution when trying to pick up something off the floor with a baby strapped on your back. Life would be a lot easier if only you still had one of those handy prehensile tails that our primate ancestors shed so casually some two million years ago.

Moored, tied, girdled, and secured to carrying devices, today's babies can safely be taken out and about. Unfortunately, proud parents who parade their newborns in well-appointed baby carriages are not necessarily giving their offspring the royal treatment. Aborigine infants who have a lot of wiggle room as they dangle in a sling against their mother's hip develop much greater motor skills than our itsy-bitsy couch potatoes who are wheeled around while reclining backward.

More than once, you'll feel like casting away all that restrictive baby gear and taking off into the world with your slippery charge straddling your midriff freestyle. Maybe you should follow this primitive urge from time to time. Though you may not get to your destination as quickly, your child will progress further and faster when riding in your arms.

But whether you are pushing a stroller or juggling a bassinet, whether you are wheeling or dandling your progeny, like the migrating hominids roaming the earth millennia ago, you will be on the move with your child. Less than a week after her birth, you will be eager to take your newborn for her first outing in the park, her first doctor's appointment, and her first official visit to close relatives and grandparents. When she's not yet a month old, you will take her along on an errand, show

Hold them tight as they wiggle their way into your heart.

her off at the office, and bundle her up for her first trip out of town. Soon you'll be her social secretary, making play dates for her to meet other babies in the neighborhood.

Children always were—and still are—a catalyst for greater mobility and increased social interaction between members of the human tribe.

The Stuff of Memories

A childhood is made of a series of fleeting moments that will linger forever in your child's unconscious. Though he will quickly outgrow his nursery environment, your baby will never completely outgrow the impression left on his psyche by his first crib, his first blanket, his first teddy bear, or his first set of wheels. Spread a touch of fairy dust on your baby's first year:

❈ Be a little extravagant when it comes to details. Have your baby announcements regally engraved on crisp, ivory-colored stationery. It's the next best thing to having a child born to royalty.

❈ Don't let anyone talk you out of getting one of those cozy quilted "Moses" baskets that will make your infant look like a baby in a manger.

❈ Splurge on an old-fashioned baby carriage that allows you to make eye contact with your newborn as you wheel her around in style.

❈ Cultivate deliberate gestures that help you savor with your baby the simple pleasures of life. Massage him with apricot oil after his bath. Take a little longer to dress him in clothes that match. Learn new nursery rhymes to lull him to sleep at night.

❈ Be sure to get a baby book to hold endearing keepsakes and mementos. In a little more than a decade, the well-worn album will be the only proof that your rebellious teenager is actually your child.

Give them a childhood worth remembering.

﹂﹃ 6 ﹄﹁

the art of bustling

ith one hundred billion hungry neurons waiting to make new connections in their brains, newborns can't afford to simply hang around. The minute they come home from the hospital, they are eager to learn new skills, like drooling all over Dad's silk tie, soiling freshly changed diapers, sticking their fingers into your eyes, grabbing jewelry, kicking the blanket over

They spill, you clean. That's the way it should be.

their heads, pulling the cat's tail, and spilling water all over the polished floor.

So small and yet so disruptive, infants generate in their wake a flutter of unexpected chores. Their utter helplessness is a call to arms. The entire household is marshaled to respond to emergencies large and small. As a result, bustling adults weave around their newborn a tireless network of domestic sounds, familiar smells, and comforting gestures.

And this activity ensures that the baby never gets bored.

Instead of thinking of your endless bustling duties as time-consuming drudgery that takes you away from the baby, think of them as a way of making your reassuring presence felt throughout the house.

As soon as the baby stops fussing, you tiptoe out of the nursery to make the rounds. Don't be upset when you realize that all the kitchen drawers are hanging open, that empty cardboard boxes are blocking the entryway, that pillows are strewn all over the living-room floor, and that dirty dishes are piled up high on the piano. By straightening up the mess, you create around your baby a comforting zone of bourgeois domesticity.

Even as she sleeps, your little girl is probably listening to you. Were you to stop moving about, she would wake up at once and call for you. But as long as you are busy, she will probably snooze peacefully.

Most likely, one of your happiest childhood memories is of nodding off at night while listening to the muffled sound of the radio, knowing that your mother was diligently doing her ironing down the hall in the laundry room.

And you probably remember being lulled into an afternoon nap by the noises your dad made raking leaves or cleaning the barbecue in the yard.

As they attend to various chores, parents send appeasing signals to their child. Your frenzied nesting symptoms in the days preceding the birth of your newborn were in fact a dress rehearsal for the friendly commotion that would take place once your baby came home.

Back then—less than a week ago!—you assumed that your sudden need to clean, scrub, and mop was just some eccentric hormonal aberration. If only you had known.

But no childcare class can ever prepare you for the challenge of simply keeping the floor clean, the sink clear, the clothes laundered, the household fed—and the baby happy.

Parenting has a lot more to do with day-to-day housekeeping than with blissful cocooning. For parents, the first few months of a baby's life are first and foremost a crash course in home economics.

THE ZEN OF GETTING THINGS DONE

You bring peace on earth as you pad about, forever putting things away, clearing out the sink, picking up the toys, wiping the counter, and mopping up the mess. All you need to do to enjoy these repetitive chores is to stop thinking of housework as a task-oriented venture.

Busy at the office right up to the time of the birth, most of us have little experience with round-the-clock housekeeping. We approach cleaning and dusting as we would setting up business objectives. We try to organize, systemize, prioritize. But with a baby in the house, we have to be willing to make plans only to cancel them. The schedule? What schedule?

The trick is to learn to be ready for anything, even when you are not ready for it.

Start by giving yourself a break. Don't decide in advance who does what, when, and where. At the end of the day, you won't get a bonus for being the one who scrubbed the tub, swept under the bed, or put the groceries away.

You will get a bonus only for remembering how lucky you are, and for taking a moment to marvel at your tiny cherub making suckling sounds.

The secret of surviving housework is simply to do it. Pull the plug on the part of your brain that always wants to negotiate everything.

You need to change a diaper, rinse a bottle, clean a spill, fluff a pillow? Consider it done. It's a no-brainer. End of conversation. End of story.

Not postponing chores—and not spending any mental energy equivocating, temporizing, or stalling—is actually a lot more restful than worrying about what needs to be done. You can breeze along, nonchalantly dispatching external clutter and internal chatter as you go.

Before long, you reach a zone of inner quietude where chasing dust bunnies can actually be as effortless as watching TV and eating bonbons.

Make your bed. See how easy it is to feel on top of the world.

Trek to the laundry room. The humming of the washing machine in its spin cycle is as relaxing as the whooshing of a Tibetan prayer wheel.

Do the dishes. The sound of running water is the next best thing to peals of laughter.

Housecleaning while a baby is resting is a mindful ritual in thanksgiving. You are not only sending germs, mites, and microbes scurrying away, but you are also turning an ordinary home into a consecrated family sanctum.

Sexy Moms

Even though you think you look like hell, you are a lot more appealing to the opposite sex than you might imagine. You have nothing left to prove as a woman, and it shows. You are looser, freer, and more candid—in a word, *sexier*.

❋ When pregnant, you look bodacious in a stretchy little black dress. Your legs are positively twiggy in contrast with your pea-in-the-pod figure. Fabulous shoes will finish the look.

❋ No baby-doll dresses or Peter Pan collars for you during—or after— pregnancy. No pastel sweatsuits either. Dark colors with bright accents (a pleated scarf, a big gold watch) will smarten up your silhouette in a minute.

❋ Cut your hair. Wear red lipstick.

❋ Spice up your conversation with racy remarks and spontaneous gestures. Roll your eyes. Wink. Blow kisses. You are a fertility goddess, not a matron—not yet.

❋ Call him "Baby, Baby." Never call him "Daddy."

❋ Too tired for sex? Not a problem. Remind him of how you got in this predicament in the first place. Then look at him with a goofy smile.

❋ Tell him you love him at least three times a week.

We've come a long way since <u>Leave It to Beaver.</u>

the art of soothing

We all assume that a baby who cries is sending distress signals. His ninety-decibel wails would make the angels weep. You pick him up, rock him, bounce him, and talk to him. If you change his diapers, if you feed and burp him, if he is neither sick nor teething, then he surely will stop howling. Yet in many instances, he doesn't.

Could those so-called distress signals mean something else entirely? With her long eyelashes drenched with tears and her tiny fists punching invisible enemies, the boohooing baby is the very picture of need. What that need is, though, is a mystery.

Research projects that try to assess the nature, duration, and patterns of postnatal cries do little to comfort worried parents. Even sophisticated acoustical analysis fails to decipher the secret language of a two-month-old's relentless screaming fits. All these scientific studies offer is the assurance that sooner or later children will outgrow their colicky stage.

The frustration of the crying infant can be compared only with the frustration of his frazzled parents who are unable to soothe him. To understand why he is in such a state, maybe they should imitate his wails and weep disconsolately to express their own grief. But in our culture, grown-ups don't cry, even when they feel like it—even when nature encourages them to do so. New mothers do their best to ignore their hormone-induced postpartum depression, with its mood swings and its cycles of self-doubt and irrational angst.

It takes months to recover from the stress of pregnancy and childbirth—about the same amount of time it takes for the baby to get over his colicky stage. But though the mother will sometimes sneak in a good cry when no one is watching, she would feel guilty if she were to shed a tear in front of her fretting newborn. Having a baby is supposed to be such a happy event. So, unlike her child, she resists indulging in sweet and salty sobs even though she would probably feel a lot better if she did.

Imagine for a moment that your baby's distress signals are sent in response to your state of mind as much as hers. She cries to compel you to get in touch with your own mounting sense of exhaustion, annoyance, and frustration. Her thin, high-pitched wails assault your senses in order to help you release your anxiety the natural way— by experiencing this altered estrogen state called baby blues.

We are responsive to our child's contagious good cheer, but we refuse to acknowledge his existential, cranky moods. When he coos, we react with appreciative oohs and ahhs. When he smiles, we grin from ear to ear. When he makes a face, we mimic his silly expression and laugh wholeheartedly. So why can't we do the same when he cries? Why can't we admit how terrified we often feel in the face of our new responsibilities?

Don't expect a three-month-old to carry alone the burden of your apprehension. Even as he fusses and kicks, find a way to let him know that you are no stranger to his misgivings. Soon he'll be

asleep in your arms, his perfect rosebud lips moist with the dew of his abbreviated tears.

A NEW FEEDING FORMULA

Before we had a child of our own, most of us assumed that crying babies had bad parents who did not attend to their needs. Now we know. With a howling infant in our arms, we don't expect anyone's sympathy. If we were toting a jackhammer, people would probably show more understanding.

Making matters worse, infants who are bottle-fed are usually a lot more irritable than babies who are breastfed. Mother's milk is a universal pacifier. A sweet elixir, it has kept infants satisfied and healthy for millennia, protecting them from hunger and infectious diseases in times of scarcity.

Two sleepy people at peace with the world.

Only during the most serious shortages of food would children be left wanting.

So irritating to our ears, the cries of babies are forever associated in our collective memory with the threat of famine. Yet for all its wondrous advantages—nutritional, immunological, and psychological—breastfeeding is not always a panacea for the mother and child. In numerous instances, kids have done better when their mothers were able to work away from home—busy in the forest or the fields, or minding the store or the office—in order to increase their family's resources.

So for crying out loud, don't feel guilty if you decide not to breastfeed. By design, human babies are highly adaptable. Their genes are coded records of their evolutionary past, not of their evolutionary future. Nature has deliberately engineered our children to be the products of nurture—of the ever-changing culture into which they are born and into which they will grow.

Today concerned parents are making use of their kids' unique adaptive qualities to negotiate what could very well be a major breakthrough in baby care. Even though they are well aware of the nutritional benefits of mother's milk, they choose not to breastfeed, or they opt for early weaning, to give men a chance to be equal players in the nurturing process.

Studies have confirmed that the more childcare tasks a dad performs on a regular basis (feeding, bathing, dressing, diapering), the smarter and more socially responsive his baby.

A mother's soothing presence is only half of the parental equation. The solace she brings to her baby by hovering constantly is well tempered by the father's growing reliability and competence. Sometimes she may choose to step back to let Dad guide their child toward independence.

Recipes for Instant Comfort

Let's hear it for melted butter. Nothing consoles a crying infant, a teething baby, or a shrieking toddler like a bowl of warm, buttery mush. The following recipes are a healthy alternative to chocolate chip cookies.

BUTTERY APPLESAUCE

Melt 1 tablespoon of butter in a heavy saucepan. Add 1 apple, peeled and quartered. Sprinkle a heaping teaspoon of sugar. Stir and add $\frac{1}{4}$ cup of water. Cover tightly. Cook 10 minutes on low heat. Let it cool, and mush with a fork to desired consistency.

BUTTERY BAKED EGG

Pour 1 tablespoon of melted butter into the bottom of an ovenproof cup. Break 1 egg into it. Top with a tablespoon of sour cream. Sprinkle grated Swiss cheese. Bake for about 15 minutes in a preheated oven at 350° F. Let it cool 5 minutes before feeding with a silver spoon.

BUTTERY BREAD MUSH

Melt 1 tablespoon of butter in a heavy saucepan. Crumble 2 slices of toasted bread into it. Sprinkle a generous teaspoon of sugar. Stir with a wooden spoon, then add some milk. Cover tightly. Cook 5 minutes over low heat. Let it cool, and mush with a fork to desired consistency. Serve in a bowl with a dollop of jelly on top.

Happiness is the smell of melting butter in a warm kitchen.

the art of negotiating

What's good for your ego is usually not good for your kid. So get over your desire to become a "proud" father or mother. Try to avoid getting into one of those three-way negotiations between you, your child, and your perfectionist self. Discipline becomes a lot easier when instead of squabbling endlessly with your little one, you argue directly with your big ego.

The will of a child is a force of nature.

Underneath our bravado, we parents are insecure—so much so, in fact, that we can never get enough reassurance. We are always on the lookout for extra approval from the countless child development specialists we meet every day—the frowning next-door neighbor, the busy janitor, the huffy flight attendant, the gruff lady at the checkout counter, the insolent delivery boy, and all the condescending nannies at the playground.

Too many of us expect our children to be well behaved so as to impress an imaginary gallery of unsuspecting strangers and regular admirers.

But our children are not gullible. Don't pretend you want them to behave for their own good. They can tell when we harbor a secret agenda, even though, most of the time, we are not aware of it ourselves. Feeling—rightly so—that the whole world is ganging up on them, kids refuse to cooperate with parents who promote them as shining reflections of themselves.

Let's say you insist your baby must go to sleep at a certain time, worried as you are that if you don't put him on a schedule, you'll attract the wrath of every childcare expert in the Western hemisphere. What happens, sure enough, is that your infant boy makes a point of never nodding off before midnight.

Let's say you try to feed your six-month-old organically grown, salt-free, hand-puréed green beans—because some mom at the playgroup remarked offhandedly that her daughter gets only home-cooked baby food. Don't be surprised if the meal turns into a scene from *The Exorcist.*

Or let's say you take your mild-mannered toddler to a fancy restaurant to introduce her to "fine dining," convinced in your heart that being a parent doesn't require that you give up your old glamorous persona. Five minutes after you sit down, your angel will treat you (and all the other patrons) to one of her most fragrant bowel movements to date.

Before they learn to speak in full sentences, most kids acquire a wide vocabulary of defensive tactics to foil our clandestine expectations. Whenever a rich relative picks them up, they howl. At fancy wedding receptions, they take off their clothes. And when they are paraded before bedtime in their brand-new pajamas, they refuse to say "nite-nite" to the dinner guests. To avoid making discipline a contest between you and your child, try to pull the rug from under your swaggering ego.

Be honest about your shortcomings. If you can't figure out how on earth you are supposed to get your two-month-old to sleep alone in her crib, say, "I give up!" and take her to bed with you.

If you can't force-feed tasteless food to your baby, say, "What the heck," and give her something she likes to eat—mashed potatoes, for instance.

And if your mate ever suggests you take your toddler to a fancy restaurant, say, "Get real." Make it your business to protect your child from snooty waiters.

GOING WITH THE FLOW

Handling the will of a baby, the tantrums of a toddler, or the misdeeds of a capricious child is like negotiating the rapids of a mountain stream. You have to hold on to your wits and paddle as fast as you can. Who knew whitewater rafting would be a good preparation for raising a kid?

Parenting is a demanding sport. If before having kids you went down the

Zambezi River in a raft, surfed twenty-foot boiling waves in the Fiji Islands, trained on the Olympic equestrian team, or tested Formula One cars for the Grand Prix, chances are you'll do great in the nursery.

When an upsurge of water hurls your inflatable boat toward a ten-foot-high waterfall, you have to go with the flow, even though your instinct is to work against the current. In the same way, when a baby wants something—his bottle, your attention, a diaper change—resistance is futile. You must satisfy his demands at once, regardless of your own needs.

Get off the sofa and pick up the baby: to feed him, to console him, to prevent him from getting hurt. Always choose action over words. Don't argue, don't complain, don't yell. Show, don't tell.

Attending to a child's daily wants is busy work indeed. But don't think of parenting as one more thing to do—think of parenting as a hundred things you don't have to worry about doing anymore. Now you have a good excuse for not going to boring parties, not running marathons, not meeting friends in noisy bars, not chairing fund-raising committees, and not signing up for another round of French conversation classes at the YMCA.

Okay, your most adventuresome days are probably over for the time being. In the back of your closet, your sleeping bag may get musty, your foul-weather gear may turn brittle, and your guitar may warp. But take heart: extreme sports and child care have a lot in common. Physical endurance. Determination. Total commitment. Once you've gone past the lip of a rapid, caught a big swell, crossed a starting line—or taken your baby home from the hospital—you can't change your mind. You are entirely in the moment, beyond fear, beyond regrets, lost in the excitement of survival.

Because I Say So

Children will always respect you if you tell them the truth. When they question the reason why you want them to behave in a certain way, don't try to bribe them, threaten them, or deceive them.

Here are a few answers you can use instead of losing your patience and declaring "Because I say so."

"Because we'll both feel better when it's over."

"Because I am running out of ideas for how to beg you to put
   your socks on."

"Because I am a lot bigger than you are."

"Because I really need you to help me get out of the house on time."

"Because I don't want the lady across the street to think that I
   am a bad mom."

"Because you don't have a better offer yet."

"Because I don't feel like getting mad at you right now."

"Because you don't want to give people who don't like kids
   more reasons to be right."

"Because you are my best friend on earth."

Don't argue. Instead offer your kid a chance to help you.

the art of celebrating

Joy. Pride. Delight. Words fail to express how you feel when you look at your child. If you weren't so tousled and tired, you'd hang banners all over the house and invite the entire neighborhood to come in and admire the chubby little addition to your family.

The love you feel for your newborn can blow your mind. Compelled by an almost organic need to

praise her qualities and virtues, you tell everyone that the little creature in your arms is absolutely the most beautiful baby on earth—taking full advantage of the fact that friends and relatives are too considerate to disagree with you.

It's a good thing your baby doesn't yet quite understand what you are saying about her.

See, children relish compliments, but they find excessive praises downright embarrassing. They want to be loved, but they also want to be liked for who they are, idiosyncrasies and all.

Even Little Lord Fauntleroy, the most perfect child in American literature, questioned whether people really liked him for himself. When throngs of birthday well-wishers came to his grandpa's castle to congratulate him on his long curls and good looks, he asked his mother, "Is it because they like me?"

Love and *like* are two different things. Though we love our children so much we would gladly give our lives to save them, we can't say we like the long hours and the tedious day-to-day reality of their growing up. In fact, our eagerness to celebrate every single milestone of their protracted childhood can be interpreted as a sign that we can't wait for it to be over.

First smiles, first words, first teeth.

And as soon as we reach these markers, we are already looking forward to the next stage—first haircut, first steps, first sticky little kiss placed on Mommy's cheek.

In the meantime, our big babies are not as eager to grow up as we assume they are. If it weren't for our constant prompting, they probably would see no reason to give up their childish ways. You can't blame them. Cool and self-possessed, they live in the moment, quite unperturbed by our wishes, hopes, and expectations for their future aggrandizement.

Maybe we should refrain from celebrating our kids' every new accomplishment and let the little devils know that we like them just the way they are.

If only for a second, we should stop looking forward to the next thing, the next chore, the next phone call, the next weekend. If we did, the sudden relaxation we'd feel in our shoulders, jaw, and thighs would alert us to the amount of tension we put into anticipating events that are yet to come.

In this nonexpectant state, we could begin to enjoy the child in front of us, from her plump fingers trying to grab an apple to the determined expression of her tiny pinched lips. And before the ticking of the clock could reclaim us, we would be able to share the present moment with her—every drawn-out minute of the day as precious as every inch of her radiant being.

SHARED HAPPINESS

In less competitive cultures, parents don't extol their children's growth the way we do. They downplay birthdays to allow each child to progress at his or her own leisurely pace.

In parts of China and Southeast Asia, for instance, birthdays are remembered as "days of continuation." In India, on the anniversary of their child's birth, mothers simply bring offerings of food to the temple as a thanksgiving gesture. And in many Catholic countries, parents still celebrate their kid's name day, rather than his birthday, to honor the patron saint after whom their child was named.

When Victorian parents introduced birthday parties for underage revelers— emulating Queen Victoria's fondness for the German *Kinderfesten* ritual—their intention

It's not enough to love kids. You also need to <u>like</u> them.

was not to celebrate the progress of the youngsters or to glorify their developing ego but to instill in them proper respect for social etiquette and good behavior.

Today you can celebrate your child's birthday without turning the event into an opportunity to teach her manners or into a rite of passage that puts extra pressure on her to grow up. As long as you design it as a chance for her to share some good cheer with her playmates, there is no harm in staging a big bash in her honor.

If it's your turn to arrange a birthday extravaganza, you spare no expense. You take half a dozen little girls in white leggings and pink tutus through Central Park in an open horse-drawn carriage. You hire a local artist to apply glittering decals around the belly buttons of shrieking toddlers. You invite a troupe of circus contortionists to perform in your backyard for a rowdy congregation of short people in short pants.

The sweets, the treats, the decorations, the treasure hunts, the costume contests, and the magic tricks are conceived only to please the diminutive hosts and their rambunctious guests, not to please you. You don't go through all this trouble in the name of love—are you kidding? If love were the issue, you would not organize an event that encourages perfectly adorable cherubs to act like a bunch of demented baby kangaroos. And you would not let them consume criminal amounts of sugar and empty calories to boot. No, the heck with love. Your kiddies' birthday parties are rituals that proclaim how much you like children.

One of the most wonderful surprises of being a parent is to find out how enjoyable it is to allow a child to be childish, even bratty at times. To accommodate his silly whims and untimely interruptions. To be understanding when she changes her mind at the last minute. To laugh with her at her most dopey jokes. And to support the fact that he relishes totally ungrown-up things such as chaos, frenzy, madness, and commotion.

Little Lord Fauntleroy, you no longer need to worry. We like you. You could get out of your pretty velvet suit. Crop your blond locks. Act goofy. Make faces. And you would still be the best little lordship on the shelves of the children's library.

A face as irresistible as a big scoop of vanilla ice cream.

Terms of Endearment

Our kids are so cute, we sometimes feel like saying, "I love you so much, I could just eat you right up."

Here is a short selection of sweet and silly terms of endearment that will establish a delicious bond of affection between you and your baby.

Angel Cake

Pumpkin

Gumdrop

Sweetie Pie

Dumplin'

Cupcake

Peanut

Honey Bun

Sugarplum

Sweet Pea

Muffin

Butter Bean

the art of
being there

You are your child's best educational toy, the only one that's not age specific. You come fully equipped, with no assembly required, no complicated operating instructions, no manufacturer disclaimer, and no chance of recall. Judged by a panel of experts as having the highest play value, you are guaranteed to stimulate and delight your offspring for years to come.

Be there—on time. It's the most sacred rule of parenting.

All you have to do is be there—and automatically your baby, your toddler, your preschooler, and your spunky preteen will feel secure enough to boldly explore the world.

And yet you fret and worry.

You want to educate your child in the very best way. Ignoring the advice of child-development experts who say that overstimulated kids don't learn faster than their more laid-back peers, you set up your newborn in a well-appointed nursery rife with interactive playthings. There you busy yourself with development video-cassettes, kiddie flash cards, and squeaky toys that promote eye-hand coordination and advanced motor skills.

You could relax. Instead of entertaining your squirmy infant with the Giggly Ladybug ABC's Teething Ring—the editor's top choice in your favorite parenting magazine—you could let the baby grab Dad's suspenders, pull Mom's ponytail, snag Grandpa's bowtie, or reach for the dog's wet nose.

Instead of trying to give your infant a leg up on the competition thanks to the latest electronic baby mindware—"it's never too early to target Harvard, Stanford, and Yale"—you could spend idle hours unlocking her creative potential by simply listening to the rain with her, playing peekaboo, or reading *Goodnight Moon* over and over.

Dream on. For many of us busy parents, the very idea of spending boundless time with a child makes us feel utterly claustrophobic.

Puttering around the house or around the neighborhood while baby-sitting can drive you bonkers.

Nothing will test your self-esteem like wiping sticky fingers, drying tears, and pushing swings and strollers.

One of the reasons stay-at-home parents keep their toddlers busy with play dates, music lessons, and art classes is to avoid going nuts.

Never mind the fact that there is no evidence that ballet classes, swimming instruction, or remedial finger-painting courses improve the academic prospects of tiny tots. Kids don't learn as much from prekindergarten extracurricular activities as we wish they did.

Furthermore, they never learn what they are supposed to learn, and they have their own quirky interpretation of what is being taught. Yet they still benefit from being taken around from class to class by their eager moms and conscientious dads.

For parents and children, doing something together is what matters. The most important learning happens when they are collaborating on a project, enjoying the same things at the same time.

🐒 Choosing the right bongo drum in a baby rhythm class.

Making new friends in a locker room while changing for toddler swim class.

Working as a team to try to figure out how to use the library vending machine.

Attempting to memorize the names of all the kids in the puppet making group.

Sharing a hot chocolate in the tea room of a fancy hotel before driving back home in the family van.

For kids, of course, the most wonderful moment is when they spot their mother cheering on the bleachers or when they catch their father's smile as they twirl on the floor. The real stuff of life, though, is the befores and afters, when their favorite grown-up shows up on time and stands by them as they pack their stuff.

THE REST OF
YOUR LIFE

It's not complicated. You are a parent; you have to plan to be available to your children twenty-four hours a day for the rest of your life.

A living link to your kids' early childhood, your job is to make sure your offspring feel eternally young. As long as you are around, in their minds they'll never grow to be as old as you are. You are their anti-aging talisman. Thanks to you, they will forever feel immune from time—their days never need to be counted.

Around Mom and Pop, even the most accomplished adults often act rather immature. Try as they might, they can't help it. At family gatherings, they are likely to start a loud argument with their siblings. When asked if they want a second helping of pie, they'll say "Fun!" instead of yes. When their father is not looking, they'll sneak a cookie to the dog. At the end of the meal, they'll tend to the fireplace in order not to do the dishes. And as their parents are ready to retire for the night, they'll suggest everyone go skinny-dipping.

So be it. The role of parents is to prolong indefinitely their kids' childhood and to ensure that, even as adults, they don't lose their connection with the most playful part of their psyche. After all, the long period of a human child's vulnerability is considered to be one of our evolutionary advantages. We are a prolific species because we never stop experimenting, goofing, and learning from our mistakes.

By reminding our children that, as long as we are around, they will always be our kids—no matter what—we urge them to surpass our wildest expectations and become much better than we are.

A Final Quiz

We want the best for our kids. But take this test before deciding that you need to make a lot of money to raise a family. As far as children are concerned, not all riches are material goods.

1. Having it all means having the wisdom not to want it all.

   True___ False___

2. Compared with raising a family, having a successful career is child's play.

   True___ False___

3. Big year-end bonuses are awarded to people who never get to tuck their kids in bed.

   True___ False___

4. The most amazing thing a father can do for his children is share the housework 50–50.

   True___ False___

5. The more guilty you feel about not being around, the more expensive the toys you'll buy for your kid.

   True___ False___

6. Quality time is not whatever time you spend with your child at the end of the day.

   True___ False___

If you hesitated before answering more than a couple of questions, you probably need to be reminded that your presence is the greatest present you can give your kids.

(Answers: 1. True; 2. True; 3. True; 4. True; 5. True; 6. True.)

If only you could turn off the phone for the next decade...

From now on, you'll see the inner child in everybody.

Before becoming a parent, you probably had strong convictions about how to raise a child. Suffice it to say that with a newborn in the house, you will be a little more subdued when voicing your opinions. Caring for a baby can turn the most self-assured among us into rather compassionate human beings.

You'll be a little more forgiving of your own limitations. You'll smile at people pushing strollers. You'll hold the elevator door for mothers with cranky toddlers. You'll volunteer to read stories to anyone wearing pajamas with feet. And chances are, you'll cry a lot more at the movies.

Eventually you'll grow to appreciate Dr. Spock's famous assertion that parents know more about baby care than they think they do. As you learn to trust yourself, you'll acquire the wisdom to avoid people and situations that make you feel guilty.

And if, from time to time, you fall prey to self-doubt, open this book to any page. You'll be reminded that you are your child's hero for a very good reason.

Brott, Armin A., and Jennifer Ash. *The Expectant Father: Facts, Tips, and Advice for Dads-to-Be.* New York: Abbeville Press, 1995.

Churchwell, Gordon. *Expecting: One Man's Uncensored Memoir of Pregnancy.* New York: HarperCollins, 2000.

Goldberg, Bonni. *The Spirit of Pregnancy: An Interactive Anthology for Your Journey to Motherhood.* Lincolnwood, IL: Contemporary Books, 2000.

Iovine, Vicki. *The Girlfriends' Guide to Pregnancy: Or Everything Your Doctor Won't Tell You.* New York: Pocket Books, 1995.

———. *The Girlfriends' Guide to Surviving the First Year of Motherhood.* New York: Berkley Publishing Group, 1997.

Karlen, Arno. *Man and Microbes: Disease and Plagues in History and Modern Times.* New York: Touchstone Books, 1996.

Martin, William. *The Parent's Tao Te Ching.* New York: Marlowe & Company, 1999.

McClenahan Burkett, Wynn. *Life After Baby: From Professional Woman to Beginner Parent.* Berkeley, Calif.: Wildcat Canyon Press, 2000.

Peri, Camille, and Kate Moses. *Mothers Who Think: Tales of Real-Life Parenthood.* New York: Pocket Books, 1999.

Ridley, Matt. *Genome: The Autobiography of a Species in 23 Chapters.* New York: HarperCollins Publishers, 2000.

Small, Meredith F. *Our Babies, Ourselves: How Biology and Culture Shape the Way We Parent.* New York: Anchor Books, 1999.

Vertosick, Frank T., Jr., M.D. *Why We Hurt: The Natural History of Pain.* New York: Harcourt, Inc., 2000.

Wright, Robert. *The Moral Animal: The New Science of Evolutionary Psychology.* New York: Vintage Books, 1995.

Front Cover: Kirsten and Desmond, St. Martin, French West Indies. *Page 2:* Empty hallway, Ruston, Louisiana. *Page 8:* Desmond in St. Martin. *Page 11:* Lilly and Nell, Brooklyn Heights, New York. *Page 12:* Late afternoon, Joshua Tree, California. *Page 16:* Winter rain, Cobble Hill, Brooklyn. *Page 19:* Fabien and Niagalé, Paris, France. *Page 21:* Stacy, Tony, and Madeleine, Brooklyn Heights. *Page 24:* Emeric and Hugo, Normandie, France. *Page 27:* Sacred hill, Louisiana. *Page 29:* Anne-Marie, Lower Manhattan. *Page 31:* Still-life with pot. *Page 32:* Anne-Marie and Jackson. *Page 35:* South Ferry, New York. *Page 36:* Royal Botanical Gardens, Sydney, Australia. *Page 40:* Daily bath. *Page 43:* Grandpapa and Hugo, Normandie. *Page 45:* Kirsten and Desmond, St. Martin. *Page 46:* Emeric with Hugo and Gaetan, Loire Valley, France. *Page 49:* Thierry with twins, Paris. *Page 50:* William, James, and Leah, East End Avenue, New York. *Page 53:* Saturday morning with Annetta and Ella. *Page 54:* Gitta and Nadia, Fort Green, Brooklyn. *Page 58:* Kirsten and Desmond, St Martin. *Pages 61 and 64:* Jackson with Mom. *Page 66:* Breakfast with Hugo, Loire Valley. *Page 69:* Nadia and Gitta. *Page 70:* View from the beach, St. Martin. *Page 74:* Emeric, Hugo, and Gaetan, Villandry, France. *Page 77:* Patrick and Luke, Park Slope, Brooklyn. *Page 80:* Isabelle and sons. *Page 82:* Dinnertime with Nadia. *Page 85:* Cypress tree, Azay-le-Rideau, France. *Page 86:* Madeleine's birthday party. *Page 90:* Kirsten and Desmond at home in Louisiana. *Page 92:* Caparra Ruins, San Juan, Puerto Rico. *Page 94:* Ella in Park Slope.

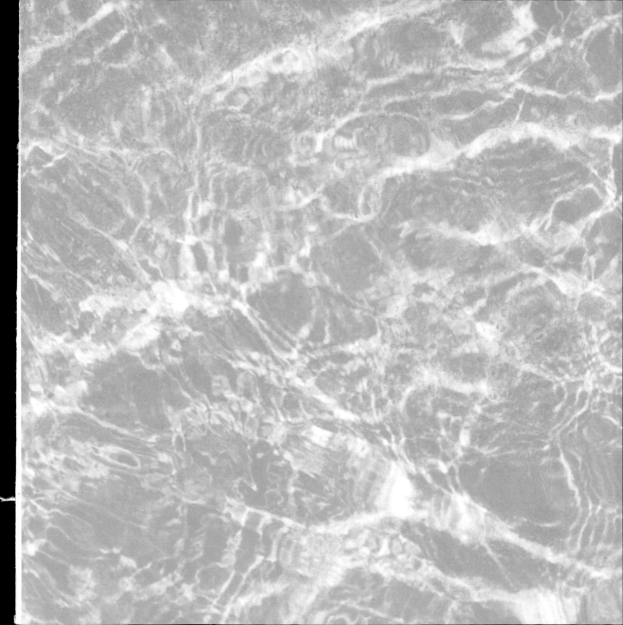